SHADES
OF PEOPLE

by **Shelley Rotner** and **Sheila M. Kelly**
photographs by **Shelley Rotner**

Holiday House / New York

To my neighbor Chiana,
who is a beautiful shade
—S. R.

For all my grandchildren, with special thanks
to my granddaughter Alexandra Lum,
who taught me that "people come
in many shades, not colors, but shades"
and provided the idea for this book.
—S. M. K.

Text copyright © 2009 by Shelley Rotner and Sheila M. Kelly
Photographs copyright © 2009 by Shelley Rotner
All Rights Reserved
HOLIDAY HOUSE is registered in the U.S. Patent and Trademark Office.
Printed and Bound in March 2023 at Toppan Leefung, DongGuan, China.
The text typeface is Montreal.
www.holidayhouse.com

25 24

Library of Congress Cataloging-in-Publication Data
Rotner, Shelley.
Shades of people / by Shelley Rotner and Sheila M. Kelly ;
photographs by Shelley Rotner. — 1st ed.
p. cm.
Summary: Explores the many different shades of human skin,
and points out that skin is just a covering that does
not reveal what someone is like.
ISBN 978-0-8234-2191-6 (hardcover)
[1. Human skin color—Fiction.] I. Kelly, Sheila M. II. Title.
PZ7.R752Shc 2009
[E]—dc22
2008022574
ISBN 978-0-8234-2305-7 (paperback)

Have you noticed that people come in many different shades?

Not colors, exactly, but shades.

There's creamy, ivory,

sandy and peach,

coffee, cocoa,

copper and tan.

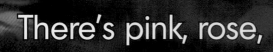
There's pink, rose,

and almond;

shades of gold,

bronze, and brown.

Some people
have skin that
is very dark;

others are pale, fair, or light.

Our skin is just our covering, like wrapping paper.

And, you can't tell what someone is like from the color of their skin.

Even in the same family

there can be many shades.

At my school
there are many
different shades.

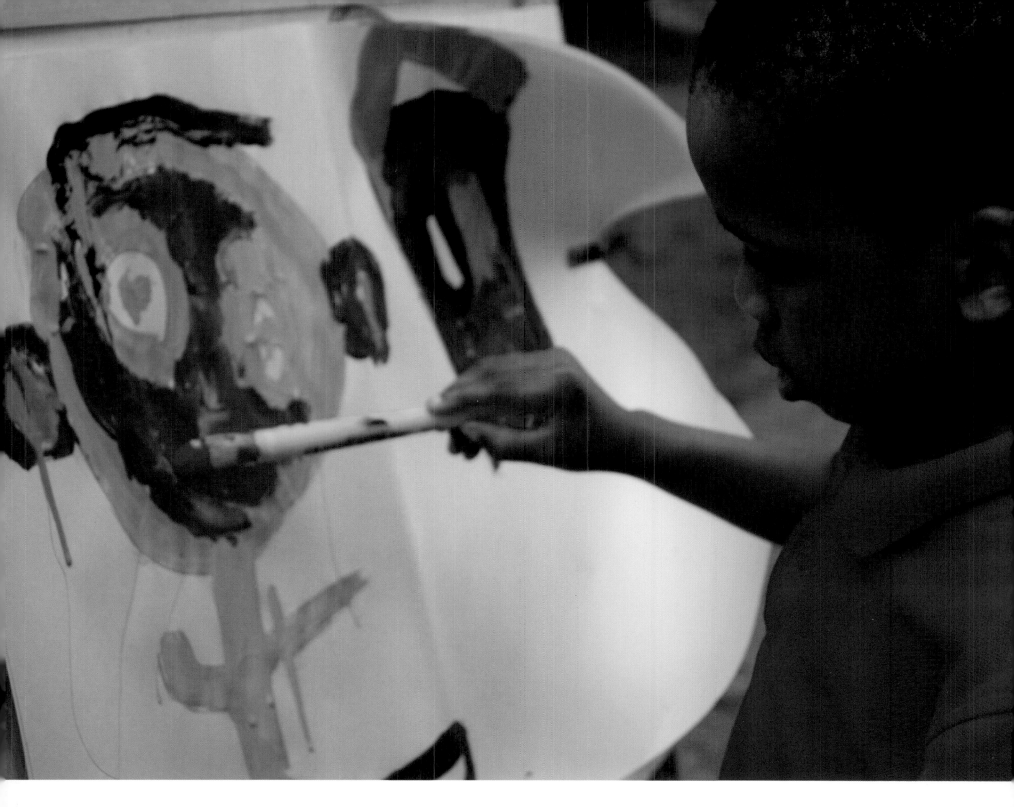

It's hard to get the right shade when I paint.

I see lots of shades at the playground

and in the park.

And at the beach too.

I see even more shades

when I'm in the city.

In the world, there's light

and dark, and everything in between.